Apples, Insights and Mad Inventors

Apples, Insights and Mad Inventors

An Entertaining Analysis of Modern Marketing

Jeremy Bullmore

John Wiley & Sons, Ltd

Other Wiley Editorial Offices

John Wiley & Sons Inc., 111 River Street, Hoboken, NJ 07030, USA

Jossey-Bass, 989 Market Street, San Francisco, CA 94103-1741, USA

Wiley-VCH Verlag GmbH, Boschstr. 12, D-69469 Weinheim, Germany

John Wiley & Sons Australia Ltd, 42 McDougall Street, Milton,
Queensland 4064, Australia

John Wiley & Sons (Asia) Pte Ltd, 2 Clementi Loop #02-01, Jin Xing
Distripark, Singapore 129809

John Wiley & Sons Canada Ltd, 22 Worcester Road, Etobicoke,
Ontario, Canada M9W 1L1

Wiley also publishes its books in a variety of electronic formats. Some
content that appears in print may not be available in electronic books.

British Library Cataloguing in Publication Data

A catalogue record for this book is available from the British Library

ISBN 13: 978-0-470-02915-2 (HB)
ISBN 10: 0-470-02915-3 (HB)

Typeset in Galliard 11/18pt by SNP Best-set Typesetter Ltd., Hong Kong
Printed and bound in Great Britain by TJ International Ltd, Padstow,
Cornwall
This book is printed on acid-free paper responsibly manufactured from
sustainable forestry in which at least two trees are planted for each one
used for paper production.

Contents

Foreword

There is no doubt that Jeremy is what the Japanese call 'a living national treasure'.

He is the best writer I've ever read – certainly on the business issues of marketing which concern every successful company. At his 60th birthday party, I unearthed his application form to join JWT in 1954 and read it out loud. The copy was as fresh, funny and insightful as it is today. If I'd been on the receiving end of his job application, I would have snapped him up. It was Jeremy at his original best. No one writes with the fluency, deftness of touch, insight and humour about the vital function of marketing as this man.

Over the years, I'm happy to say, our WPP annual reports have attracted a good deal of praise and recognition. For the last eight of those years, Jeremy's essays have made an elegant contribution – deftly complementing the hard information and the evocative design. I'm delighted that these pieces are now being brought to a wider audience through this collection. They have a timeless value.

Sir Martin Sorrell, CEO, WPP

About the Author

Jeremy Bullmore was born in 1929. He went from school to National Service, then to Oxford where he spent two years not reading English. His first job, in 1954, was as a trainee copywriter with JWT in London, and he stayed with that agency until his retirement in 1987. He became successively copywriter, writer/producer, creative group head and head of television; then from 1964 to 1975, head of the creative department and from 1976 to 1987, chairman, London. He was a member of the JWT worldwide board and, from 1981 to 1987, chairman of the Advertising Association.

He was a non-executive director of the Guardian Media Group from 1988 to 2001. Having been a non-executive director of WPP since 1988, he stepped down in September 2004 to join the WPP Advisory

Board. He is currently president of the Market Research Society. He continues to write and speak regularly about advertising and marketing and is a regular columnist for *The Guardian, Campaign, Management Today* and *Market Leader*. He was awarded a CBE in 1985.

He is married to Pamela, a garden designer and writer. They have three grown-up children and live in London and Wiltshire.

Jeremy Bullmore's other books include *Another Bad Day at the Office?, More Bull More: Behind the Scenes in Advertising (Mark III)* and *Ask Jeremy.*

Introduction

Feona McEwan is Director of Communications at WPP and one her many responsibilities is the creation and production of the Annual Report and Accounts. About nine years ago, she suggested that the report should carry an essay on some aspect of marketing communications. It became a tradition.

The eight short pieces in this book appeared in eight consecutive WPP annual reports: the first in the Report for 1997, the last in the Report for 2004. Here, they are collected together for the first time.

Six of the eight were written specifically for the Reports, though they were all reprinted later in *Market Leader. Posh Spice & Persil* started life as the second British Brands Group Lecture. And *Why Is a Good Insight Like a Refrigerator?* was in large part derived from a Keynote Address to the Market Research Society annual conference in March 2005. The earlier essays are also to be found in *More Bull More*, published by the World Advertising Research Center (WARC) and reprinted with its permission.

Some themes recur.

Polishing
the Apples

Why Successful Businesses Need Sherpas,
Machine Oil and Global Positioning Systems

It's always a good question to put to a new client: we all know what you make – but are you as certain what your customers are buying?

Simple as it sounds, it's a constructively difficult question to answer.

You make expensive pens; but that's not what people are buying. What people are buying will be prestige, or personal pleasure, or the hope of gratitude from a recipient.

You make multi-coloured chocolate buttons; but that's not what people are buying. What people are buying is a moment's welcome peace from demanding children.

3

You make laptop PCs; but that's not what
people are buying. What people are buying will
be self-sufficiency, self-esteem, efficiency and
mobility.

As Theodore Levitt pointed out many years ago:
people don't want a quarter-inch drill; they want a
quarter-inch hole. And for every product or service,
there's an equivalent distinction to be made –
though seldom so easily or so elegantly.

So it was time, it seemed to us, to ask exactly the
same question of ourselves. We know what we make,
all right: what we produce. But what is it exactly
that our clients are buying?

Here are some of the more familiar 'products' of the
marketing services industry: advertisements, tracking
studies, market analysis, strategic counsel, retail
interiors, corporate videos, annual reports, corporate
identities and liveries, sales promotions, media,
database marketing, pack designs, employee

communications, public relations and public affairs advice.

Worldwide expenditure on all marketing services in 1997 was estimated at almost $1 trillion. The outlook suggests more-or-less steady growth in such expenditure and the figure represents the aggregate of millions of different decisions voluntarily made by millions of individuals in millions of different competitive enterprises. So it can presumably be assumed that marketing companies, with attitudes ranging from cheerful confidence to resigned reluctance, believe their marketing expenditures to be necessary.

But, as with Ted Levitt's drill, nobody wants to buy advertisements or research reports for their own sakes, to be kept proudly behind glass in the corporate lobby. As with Ted Levitt's drill, all these products are bought in the hope that they will do something: to provide the equivalent of Ted Levitt's hole. Precisely what that something is, and how it differs from service to service, is a great deal harder to identify and articulate. To say that they are bought by companies to make themselves more successful is both true and unhelpful. It tells us what these services are expected to achieve but not how.

It would take a full-length book to do justice to the subject. Each service, each discipline, has a different function, often complementary; most have many more than one; and the functions may change for each client company or each brand over time.

What this brief essay sets out to do is to probe just a little beneath the surface, and try to identify some of the underlying needs that marketing services meet: for most client companies, most of the time.

So we will practise what we preach, and start with the consumer. And in WPP's case, of course, our immediate consumers are our clients.

WPP's 50 companies serve some 15,000 clients: and they are all different. They have perhaps just one thing in common:

They all need to put a competitive case; and they all want to do it cost-effectively.

The need 'to put a case' means the need to communicate, by whatever means, with a wider group. And this holds true for repeat purchase consumer goods, for capital goods, for charities, for financial services, for personnel recruitment, for business to business, for media.

Within their own sectors, they are all in open competition and they are all seeking to enhance their competitive positions.

It is kindergarten stuff to say that, if a company sets out to improve its profitability, it has only two distinct areas of action open to it: not as alternatives,

but as different approaches. It can minimise costs
and it can maximise value.

But one way to clarify the contribution of
marketing services is to ask: which are the
disciplines that help client companies minimise
costs; which are the ones that help client
companies maximise value; and which, if any, can do
both?

The first function of market knowledge, for example,
is to minimise subsequent marketing waste. Before
you can begin to put a competitive case, you need
to know your market, what your prospective
consumers think of you, what they think of your
competitors, what their misconceptions are, what
they know and what they think they know. Without
such knowledge, you'll be transmitting blind. You'll
be reaching the wrong people with the wrong
appeals: and that's a waste of time and a waste of
money. Worse, you'll almost certainly be making the
wrong product.

In the same way, money spent on the monitoring of your communications as you go along does not of itself add value to those communications: but it's the only way to identify error and so make subsequent expenditure more efficient.

The product that's sold is called *Research*.

The product that's bought is more like a global positioning system, feeding back to its owner immensely valuable knowledge of competitive position, progress and direction.

The value of employee communications is finally beginning to get the recognition it deserves. When a company decides to achieve new efficiencies through restructuring itself, it may feel like strong leadership – it may even feel efficient – to impose radical change overnight by means of a couple of all-staff memoranda sent down from the bridge. But employees who haven't been consulted, haven't been informed and feel that they haven't even been thought about can be immensely expensive obstacles to change: not because they're ill-intentioned but because they're ill-informed. Ill-informed people quite naturally become apprehensive and resistant. And the consequential costs, though difficult to quantify, will always be high: in the greatly extended implementation process; in the loss of good people; in the general decline in morale. A sustained program of listening, consultation, conversation and information can minimise confusion and hesitation, build trust through understanding, and contribute usefully to a sense of corporate unity.

The product that is sold is called *Employee Communications* or *Internal Marketing*.

The product that is bought is more like machine oil: at small extra expense, lubricating the process of comprehension and willing compliance swiftly and smoothly throughout the organisation.

10

There are other marketing services that fulfil much the same function. Before you start doing business in a country unfamiliar to you, you will need to know how best to put your case. And that means getting to know the laws and customs of that country; the language of that country; the opinion formers of that country; and the media of that country.

The product that is sold is called *Public Affairs.*

The product that is bought is more like a mountain guide: an experienced Sherpa who's scaled that peak before and knows where all the crevasses are.

The central virtue of direct marketing – relationship marketing – is its ability to separate the more valuable consumers from the less valuable consumers and concentrate effort and ingenuity on those with the greatest potential. It is an immensely accurate and efficient approach.

The product that is sold is called *Direct Marketing*.

The product that is bought is more like a prospector's sieve, screening out the mud and waste and exposing the few bright glints of gold for all to see.

All those, and there are many more, are examples of marketing services whose primary but not exclusive value lies within the broad category of contributing to efficiency through saving costs: in many cases, as a result of saving time.

But it's at least as much for the second category – for their ability to add value to brands and services – that client companies look to marketing services.

Wherever consumers have both money and choice, an intrinsically good product offering gives a marketing company no more than permission to compete. Winning will depend on its ability to add greater value than competitors can: and part of that value will come from presentation. To put a competitive case is to present your case – your company, your product, your idea, your policies, your proposition – as attractivelyas possible.

It's why people buy cosmetics, why window-dressers should be well paid and why costermongers polish their apples.

No competitive enterprise, in whatever field of endeavour, can leave its apples unpolished and still expect to win. There may still be a few who belong to the 'good wine needs no bush' school of marketing but they won't be found amongst the winners and quite soon they won't be found at all.

There are those who accept the need for pack design but believe that its only function is to make the product 'stand out on shelf'. It should certainly do that; but it should also do a great deal more.

There was much talk a few years back about the coming domination of something called 'generic brands'. As a phrase, it was a contradiction in terms. As a concept, it had limited consumer appeal. But it's instructive to remember just how institutional 'generic' packaging was: like State-approved commodities in State-owned stores in corporatist regimes.

A brand, to be successful, needs to be singular; needs to have a personality; needs to engage the heart as well as the mind. A good pack can synthesise and express all this in a way that no other medium can – and will continue to give added pleasure to its consumers throughout the product's life.

What design companies sell is called *Pack Design*.

But what clients buy is more like a brand's identity card: its DNA, in telling, graphic form.

For a company, its pack-shot will be its letter-
heading, its symbol: a unique combination of words
and design that comes to represent the whole.

What design companies sell is called *Corporate
Identity*.

But what clients buy is more like a national flag or
football strip: an instantly recognisable rallying-
point, that can absorb and retransmit the values and
achievements of the whole.

And then there is advertising, which has almost as
many roles and functions as it has users. But
probably its most common use – and the one most
likely to puzzle both financial directors and social
commentators – is that of supporting and promoting
established brands and services. People can accept
the need for advertising when launching a brand or
having made an improvement to a brand – but find
it harder to see the value in spending money to tell

people about the existence of something they very possibly already use. And it is here that we need to recognise the value of celebrity.

Celebrity is recognised by theatrical agents and promoters and publicists as having a necessary value for people. It has an equivalent value for brands.

Indeed, George W S Trow has written: 'The most successful celebrities are products.'

Being around, being well known, being salient, being contemporary – in any market – are vital preconditions for sustained competitive success. But these qualities, like suntan, fade over time. They need, constantly, to be refreshed. And that is precisely what much of the best advertising for established brands is doing – year in, year out.

What agencies sell is called *Advertising*.

But what client companies buy is more like a pool of spotlight on a stage; a trickle recharge for a brand's batteries; or a lasting place in the Hall of Fame.

The demand for communications services continues to grow: and so does the range of such services. Though existing media may be forced to reposition themselves with the arrival of new ones, no marketing medium has yet been totally superseded. So the choice available to the enterprise with a competitive case to put grows ever wider – and potentially ever more bewildering.

In evaluating the new ones, and in ensuring that the chosen disciplines work together with consonance and coherence, one final metaphor may help.

There are two forces at work when you try to make progress: Thrust and Drag.

Some of our products help their client-consumers reduce Drag, and some help their client-consumers increase Thrust – and some do both.

If they are selected, bought and evaluated not for what they are but for what they do, the management of marketing can seem a great deal less complicated.

Time-and-Motion Man
and
The Mad Inventor

ll evidence suggests that successful companies become and remain successful by adopting two apparently contradictory policies. They then insist that these two policies cohabit in conditions of mutual respect and are meticulous in never consistently favouring one at the expense of the other.

They have no commonly accepted names, but one of the best and earliest descriptions of them comes from E F Schumacher's 1973 classic, *Small Is Beautiful*. In a passage about corporate organisation, Schumacher writes:

"Without order, planning, predictability, central control, accountancy, instructions to the underlings, obedience, discipline – without these nothing fruitful can happen, because everything disintegrates. And yet – without the magnanimity of disorder, the happy abandon, the *entrepreneurship* venturing into the unknown and incalculable, without the risk and the gamble, the creative imagination rushing in where bureaucratic angels fear to tread – without this, life is a mockery and a disgrace."

Here, wonderfully well evoked, are the two nameless and apparently contradictory policies. In honour of Schumacher, they might be known simply as Order and Disorder but that hardly does them justice. I like to think of them as Time-and-Motion Man and The Mad Inventor.

We know them both well, of course. But because the human mind finds paradox uncomfortable, we feel we need to side with one of them at the expense of the other: we cannot, we believe, be best friends with both. And we find it quite impossible to imagine that they could ever be partners – as indeed, it has to be said, do they. It is Time-and-Motion's conviction that Mad Inventors have no place whatsoever in well-ordered corporate affairs; and every Mad Inventor knows that Time-and-Motion means the death of creativity and enterprise.

It was Schumacher's great contribution to point out that much of good management consists in the reconciling and balancing of conflicting demands – while still retaining the ability to function; in much the same way, he said, as the successful management of societies consists in reconciling and balancing the conflicting demands of individual liberty and social cohesiveness. In theory, it seems impossible. In practice, we manage it every day.

The importance of Time-and-Motion Man to competitive business hardly needs rehearsing: and recessions and rumours of recessions remind us of it all the time. To achieve and maintain a low-cost base; to buy efficiently; to concentrate your points of manufacture; to manage money; to look always for less labour-intensive ways of doing things: to become leaner and meaner. No manager can doubt that, to have even a chance of sustained success, today's competitive companies must be constant in their employment of the Time-and-Motion Man: "Planning, central control, accountancy, discipline – without these, everything disintegrates." Without these, you're dead.

And so the legitimate demands of Time-and-Motion Man have influenced company structures, company cultures – and company policies on recruitment and reward. Efficiency is honoured, waste is deplored; and quite right, too.

The mistake, of course, without budging for a moment from one's total commitment to Time-and Motion Man, is to believe that he is the only employee we need. And there are good reasons to believe that, in 1999, this could be a bigger mistake than at any time in commercial history.

Commentators are surprisingly agreed. Business – and businesses – are changing fast. There is a new alchemy around. Two 20-year-olds in a garage, without access to capital or raw materials or plant, can found a company that within 25 years will become the world's biggest.

Where once there was an industrial age, and then an information age, we're now well into the age of the imagination: an age where the price and availability of knowledge and technology may favour the small over the large; the innocent over the experienced; the bold over the cautious; the inventive (and frequently wrong) over percentage-playing consolidators. An age where something called intellectual capital can make a nonsense of conventional balance sheets.

The nature of risk has changed, too. Because new thoughts can be test-flown so quickly, it may be a great deal more risky to do nothing than to do something. Too many management careers are still driven by the need to circumnavigate failure. In Silicon Valley, early failure is seen as evidence of enterprise and a necessary qualification for future support.

What all these changes are doing is to put an even greater premium on the value of ideas: product ideas, process ideas, distribution ideas, positioning ideas, brand extension ideas, communications ideas.

So increasingly, companies must look to their cultures and structures; because the structures and cultures that were installed at the insistence of Time-and-Motion Man are often hostile to challenge and unorthodoxy; to the free-thinking generation of new hypotheses; to the kind of habitat in which The Mad Inventor will flourish most productively.

The Mad Inventor invents indiscriminately; and will promote his bad ideas as relentlessly as his good ones. He has only to hear of an accepted practice to know that it needs to be overthrown. He is vain, unreliable, and whimsical in his judgments. He despises timesheets. But The Mad Inventor – at least some of the time – is challenging the conventional, teasing out hypotheses, forging new connections, making new analogies – and haphazardly scattering seeds; some of which, in a few years' time, will become the harvest on which the whole of his organisation lives.

The happier he is in his habitat, the more fertile he will be. He does not respond gracefully to insistent micro-management by Time-And-Motion Man. If he feels the constraints of the corporate straitjacket, he will not succumb meekly and catch his usual 6.14 home. He will leave; even if he has nowhere else to go.

In his 1996 book *The Hungry Spirit*, Charles Handy echoes Schumacher: "Creativity needs a bit of untidiness. Make everything too neat and tidy and there is no room for experiment. Keep a tight rein on costs and there is no cash available to try new things or new ways. Cram your days too full and it's hard to find time to think. We all need a bit of slack to give us the space to experiment."

All good marketing case-histories celebrate the contribution of a great idea. But you can read a thousand and still be left wondering how great ideas happen. You will read about the market analysis that was done, the conclusions that were drawn, the strategy that was adopted. And then it says something like: "And so the Giant Platypus was born." Two thousand words later we will have learned how the Giant Platypus has increased brand share by 10 percentage points and profits by several million – but the one thing we will not have learned is how the Giant Platypus came into being in the first place.

The idea may be a product idea, a positioning idea, a communications idea. You may be certain of only one thing: the precise circumstance of its emergence will remain forever unknown and unchronicled. And so it is always bound to be.

It is no good instructing Time-and-Motion Man to install procedures designed to optimise idea production on schedule and within budget. As Schumacher, Handy, and the chief executives of marketing communications companies know only too well, that is not the way that ideas happen. Increasing the quantity and quality of ideas is partly about recruiting a Mad Inventor or two – and at least as much about creating an environment in which Mad Inventors are honoured.

Commercial communications companies – advertising, design, public relations – are unusual. Their only raw material is information and their only manufacturing facility is the human brain. Data is delivered to the back door; is subjected to analysis, experience and interpretation; and is then transformed, after intense exposure to the imagination, into An Idea. These are companies who for all their lives have recognised the claims of both Time-and-Motion Man and The Mad Inventor; and have enjoyed some modest success in learning how to manage them.

The trick, of course, is to know when in the creative process to give precedence to each. There are times for rigour and there are times to fly.

And it is this experience, surely, that could be of far greater value to client companies in the future. If a conscious application of the imagination is to be extended into the corporate whole, if company strategy is to be as creative as corporate communications strive to be, then it would seem to make sense to adopt similar planning procedures.

Time-and-Motion and The Mad Inventor

The first stage is the selection and analysis of all
relevant information: What is our current situation?
How do we seem to our customers? How do we
stand competitively? Do we see trends – and if so, in
which direction? No room for whimsy, here. No
room for guesswork or flair or approximations: just
hard, rigorous, clinical interrogation. For outside
advisers, the client company may well look to the
management consultant. Time-and-Motion Man is
in his element.

Then: What is possible for the future? What is our
most desirable (practical) destination? Subtly, the
rules of engagement change – because there's now a
need for speculation. The Mad Inventor, until now
on the benches, is called on to the field.

If invited to speculate, Time-and-Motion man
becomes unhappy. He is interested in a destination
only if he can see immediately how to get there. By
contrast, the Mad Inventor finds speculation
irresistible – and can become irrationally committed

to a destination whether or not there is discernible access to it. Between them, skilfully managed, an hypothesis is formed. Given the technology, given our knowledge and our foresight: this is where we could be.

And then finally: How do we get there? What actions, deeds, changes, inventions, investments do we need to make that will make our arrival at that destination most probable?

This, with a small roll of drums, is The Mad Inventor's big moment. Because it is now that we need "the magnanimity of disorder, the happy abandon, the *entrepreneurship* venturing into the unknown and the incalculable . . ." It is at this moment (for the moment) that Time-and-Motion Man should be gagged and bound and left in the locker room. And where the advertising agency, the design consultant or the public relations counsel could be involved and motivated and encouraged to think irresponsible thoughts; to supplement internal corporate resource; to augment "the creative imagination rushing in where bureaucratic angels fear to tread."

Ideas do not have to be good ideas to be useful. Thinking impossible thoughts has a value. The deliberate suspension of censorious judgment may be the only way to liberate minds from the deeply-rutted convictions of earlier times. The imagination flies free.

And then, of course, comes the final stage. The flying is over and rigour returns. Time-and-Motion Man is released from his bonds. Assessment begins.

But the scope of the opportunities and the richness of the landscape ahead will far exceed anything that a more responsible, methodical, deductive approach might have generated. And more efficiently, too; and a great deal more enjoyably.

As business learns to compete in the new creative age, the efficient exploitation of the imagination will be as critical to success as the exploitation of coal once was. And it would be good to think that some of the management skills and tricks that its communications advisers have painfully accumulated over the years could be brought more usefully and centrally to bear.

There are two final points to be made about Time-and-Motion Man and The Mad Inventor. They do not, of course, have to be men. And even more importantly, they do not even have to be two people. In most of us, there are traces of both Time-and-Motion Man and Mad Inventor; though some of us may have a great deal more of one than the other. If the phrase 'managing the imagination' means any one thing, it is the ability to value both; to honour both; and to know when, as ringmaster, to give each of these star performers top billing.

Why Every Brand
Encounter Counts

Seductive, Anarchic or Catastrophic

You read a compelling advertisement for a piece of electrical equipment and you buy it. And then you open the instruction manual.

It is incomprehensible in seven languages.

The advertisement understood the reader; the manual does not. In design and empathy, the brand of the advertisement and the brand of the manual have nothing whatever in common. For the purchaser, those first moments of ownership are crucial. Critical faculties are on full alert; apprehension lurks; reassurance is anxiously awaited. And that's exactly when the dreaded manual strikes.

Not only has a perfect opportunity been lost to confirm new users in the wisdom of their choice, but a perverse and wilful act of brand mutilation has been committed.

For the best part of 50 years now, we've spoken confidently about brand image and brand reputation. Nobody has seriously challenged the view that people hold opinions about products and services that are based on more than function and direct experience. This shared understanding has helped shape and improve all conventional marketing communications: no-one much doubts that advertising, direct marketing, promotions, public relations and pack design, among others, can enhance the reputations of competitive enterprises (they don't have to be objects) to the benefit of buyers and sellers both.

Where we've been less assiduous – perhaps because we sense the quest would be such a nightmare – is in trying to identify the less obvious sources of a brand's reputation.

Imagine for a moment that it was possible to scan the human brain, isolate the cell that contained that particular brain's opinion of a particular brand – its image – and then trace and log its origins. Not for one second should we expect to see just a few strong, clearly differentiated wires labelled Experience, Advertising, Word-of-Mouth, Presentation. If we successfully traced and identified every encounter that had contributed over time to that brain's view of that brand, the resultant three-dimensional map would be like a huge bowl of multi-coloured spaghetti: too complex, too confusing, too inter-related to be of any immediate value.

But that's no reason for pretending that they don't exist. The non-conventional contributors to brand reputation are already more important than we admit – and every social and technological change is making them more so. With greater understanding of these less famous brand ingredients, and some canny management, a real opportunity for competitive advantage presents itself; and at virtually no cost.

In surveying the entire range of brand encounters, we can identify two clear and coincident scales: one of simplicity and one of control. The communications we favour – and will rightly continue to favour – are relatively simple both to manage and to monitor.

Advertising, direct marketing, pricing, promotions, public relations, sponsorship, packaging, the brand website, in-store display – all in different ways and at different times affect any single individual's impression of a brand. As marketers, we take them all seriously, pay more than lip-service to the concept of integrated communications and strive hard to see that the signals that each activity sends out are consistent, coherent and complementary.

All these activities, diverse as they are, have much in common. They are all planned, paid for and executed by the brand's owners. Control, of both quantity and content, lies with the company. They are all transmissions: broadcast from the company to its consuming public. They are deliberately engineered brand encounters; and, as encounters go, they are seductive in nature. Their primary intention is to court custom. This form of brand communication is at least a thousand years old: as old as the Town Crier and probably older.

Town Crier publicity brings news to the people. It may be difficult to plan and expensive to execute but its value has never been more widely recognised. Demand for all forms grows in real terms, year by year. It will continue to be the basis of reputation for any competitive enterprise, from candy bars at 25¢ to executive cars at $100,000. It will continue to be the first serious marketing investment made by every internet debutant.

So valuable are these simple, controllable conventional encounters that it's tempting to believe that they are the only contributors to brand reputation – and all that efficient brand management entails is sitting high up in the corporate palace monitoring brand transmissions worldwide for relevance and consistency.

But there are other sources – many other sources – from which we as consumers derive our opinion of brands. Some of them are within the control of the company (though not necessarily of brand management); and some of them lie almost completely outside management control and influence. They're getting more numerous and more important every day that passes – but so fragmented are they, crossing and challenging traditional corporate structures and budgets, that many companies choose not to think about them at all.

So first, a look at some of those brand encounters which technically lie within the company's control, yet only rarely seem to be consciously directed or monitored. It is as if we believe that only conventional communications will be noted by our publics and that all other encounters will be screened out. But no manifestation of a brand is ever ignored; and all will make some contribution, positive or negative, to that brand's reputation.

The ill-conceived and incomprehensible instruction manual is one such example. But there are many other brand encounters which differ from seductive encounters in that they all have a reason for existence other than the courtship of the consumer. It's just such a pity that this primary function so often seems to blind companies to their potential for simultaneous (and free) brand-building.

It is odd how little brand use is made of trucks. Vast travelling billboards, already paid for, thunder up and down the highways being seen by hundreds of thousands of people: yet with little or nothing on their sides to promote or enhance the company or the brand. Can it be, in the corporate structure, that trucks come under transport rather than communications? And who is a transport manager to know about brand values?

The contribution of architecture to corporate brands is widely debated but infrequently practised. At a time when all are agreed that corporate brands need to be as clearly differentiated one from another as repeat-purchase consumer goods, tens of millions can be committed to buildings and internal design without a single reference made to the likely effect on the ultimate customer. It is as if senior management believes that creating a competitive reputation can safely be left to the hired hands in the marketing department and is nothing whatever to do with them.

Financial services companies were slow to understand the need for simple brand distinction –

but they're catching up fast. Savings schemes and
pension plans are now packaged far more attractively
and the language in which they are described is
sometimes even coherent. But then you get a letter
from head office – and your conclusion is immediate.
The presentation was a sham, no more than cosmetic.
Behind that glossy package lies a company as
bureaucratic, self-obsessed and insensitive as we
always knew such companies to be. In its advertising –
in its planned, seductive encounters – a large British
financial institution makes much of its friendliness.
But a recent head office communication from the
same company contained the following sentence:
"This is a computer-generated message and therefore
has no signature."

The fury provoked by poorly-trained people in call
centres and by interminable pass-the-parcel voice-
mail systems has been widely reported. But until
somebody quantifies the cost of that fury and the
damage it does to a company's bottom line, little
improvement is likely.

These are wasted opportunities: contacts between brand and brand user which have to happen; which are within the company's control; but because their primary function is other than brand communication, are thought to have no brand effect. The majority of marketing companies do not think of them as media; do not monitor them as media; and therefore make no attempt to integrate them with more conventional media. Their customers, however – their buying public – make no such distinction. And so substantial sums of money, which could have reinforced brand values from unexpected directions, are at best under-utilised and at worst counter-productive. There are many more brand encounters of this kind – all essentially anarchic in nature. By failing to confirm the brand's true spirit, they challenge it: and so brand authority is needlessly diminished.

Even more slippery to deal with, but with even greater future implications, are the chance encounters.

Just as we bump into friends and relations, so we bump into brands. These accidental interfaces are almost completely outside the control or influence of the brand owner – but their effect on the public can be significant. Because they are so disparate and diffuse, chance encounters seldom earn a mention in a communications strategy document. Because they are almost impossible to foresee, control or orchestrate, they tend to be totally ignored.

Here are just a few examples.

A story in the press about racial discrimination at a brand's factory; a meeting with a friend who has a friend who's just been sacked by the company that makes the brand; a crusading website devoted to your company's pay policy in the Middle East; a product recall for safety reasons; a cardboard outer, bearing the brand name, in an untidy corner of a supermarket; dangerous driving by a clearly-branded truck; rumoured financial problems at the holding company; a scare story started by an industrial blackmailer; a discarded wrapper in a well-tended park; a widely-reported case against the company for sexual discrimination; two cars, of the same make, broken down on the roadside within a mile of each other.

You could add another hundred: the majority trivial, a few potentially catastrophic. Most chance encounters are negative in impact; and every single one of them will have some lasting effect on people's aggregate belief in a brand – and therefore on its success and profitability.

Every change that's taking place today increases both the number and the effect of such unhappy accidents.

The age of the free-standing brand is nearly over. For reasons widely understood, most brands now – and nearly all new brands – trumpet the name of their parent. The parent may be a company or a master brand but the reasoning is the same: let's leverage our brand equity; let's trade on the trust we've already so painstakingly and expensively built.

But of course, just as the good news can be shared and spread through such linkages, so can the bad. Free-standing brands – orphan brands, with no known parents – may be non-contagious. But when brand relationships are not just public but widely publicised, bad news from one can rapidly become an epidemic.

The effect of the internet is to accelerate the chances of brand contagion. The internet means that there is nowhere to hide. You cannot charge $350 for a pair of chinos and pay third world workers $3.50 a day to make them and hope to go unnoticed. You cannot deprive your own workforce of knowledge of your company's performance when they have ready access to it elsewhere.

Today, to a marked extent, all brands are service brands. Other than street traders, few businesses now see their only function as being simply to make a sale. After-sales service, relationship marketing, the concept of lifetime value, the growth of interactive media: all these trends and developments mean that a few unfortunate chance encounters can poison a consumer's mind for ever – and undo the effect of all those seductive encounters so expensively engineered by the marketing department.

The one great certainty about all long-term relationships, of course, is that they go through rocky patches. The maintenance of immaculate service standards is even harder to achieve than the maintenance of product standards. Errors are inevitable. But if chance encounters are really chance, and lie well outside a company's sphere of control, surely that means that there is no sensible corrective action the company can take?

But there is. In this new and open commercial world, future prizes will go not just to those who make the fewest errors – but also to those who recover, apologise and make amends most gracefully. There is ample evidence that a brand that takes corrective action quickly and sympathetically will not only be forgiven but may well, as a result, find itself even more thoroughly trusted.

And it is here that the great neglected army of the workforce demands new attention. When nearly all brands are service brands; when it is the people behind the brand who provide the long-term reassurance; when news and information about brands is freely accessible from the internet and elsewhere; and when the gracious correction of inevitable error becomes a competitive necessity: that's when an intelligent, informed and trusted staff can turn even the catastrophic brand encounter into a reinforcement of brand loyalty.

This means opening up the whole marketing strategy to absolutely everyone. It means confiding in them and training them and asking them for constructive suggestions. It means trusting them to respond to customer dissatisfaction both immediately and personally, without cowering behind head office instructions. It means as conscious an application of internal marketing – internal communications – as we give to our external marketing.

Sometimes mesmerised by the new media, we neglect to make full use of the old. Whether seductive, anarchic or catastrophic, the number of brand encounters can only multiply. Each one is an opportunity. But to make the most of them, the function of Brand Management needs to be radically redefined.

The Clipboard
and the
Copywriter

*— and why the uncalculable can be
of incalculable value*

Many years ago, when cost accounting and efficiency experts were enjoying disproportionate popularity, a man with a clipboard interviewed an advertising agency copywriter.

"Tell me," said the clipboard, pencil poised, "How long does it take to write a thirty-second commercial?"

The copywriter, a seasoned survivor of difficult client meetings, didn't hesitate.

"Two hours and twenty-three minutes," he replied.

The expert nodded, made a note and moved on. He later counted up the number of commercials written by the agency in the course of a year, multiplied the figure by two hours and twenty-three minutes, divided the total by the number of copywriters on the payroll: and concluded in his written report that 48 per cent of them were surplus to requirements.

He may well, of course, have been right – but if so, through chance rather than calculation.

The WPP annual report and accounts for the year 2000 contains approximately 7,500 numbers. They attempt to do far more than comply with the company's legal and fiduciary obligations. They strive to convey, with forensic accuracy, the anatomy of the business that its shareholders own; its scope; its competitive performance; its 80-plus component parts; and all this broken down by region and discipline.

It is absolutely no criticism of these figures, nor of those who painstakingly compiled and audited them, to say that, while they accurately quantify the bone-structure of the company, they fail almost completely to evoke its essential character.

Of course we need numbers. Without numbers, incoherence reigns, progress goes uncharted, comparisons become impossible and a company's value is literally incalculable. The danger of numbers is not that they exist but that we become mesmerised by them; that we come to believe that the importance of things is directly related to their susceptibility to measurement.

In his book *The Tyranny of Numbers*, David Boyle quotes the economist Robert Chambers:

"Quantification brings credibility. But figures and tables can deceive, and numbers construct their own realities. What can be measured and manipulated statistically is then not only seen as real; it comes to be seen as the only or the whole reality." And Chambers summed it all up like this:

"Economists have come to feel
What can't be measured isn't real.
The truth is always an amount –
Count numbers; only numbers count."

Coming to feel that only numbers count is seductive. Numbers seem so safe and scientific. Numbers protect us from making subjective judgments that may be open to challenge. Numbers are like security blankets. But in our heart of hearts, we already know that not everything that matters can be quantified: so we look for ways to measure the immeasurable. In certain competitive sports, judges ascribe a score to something called artistic excellence. You might as well mark a Monet out of ten.

We look, in other words – however uneasily – for ways to quantify quality. Today there are numbers being attached to ethical behaviour and corporate citizenship. It's probably better than ignoring them altogether, but the numbers are not true numbers, like the number of metres in a kilometre; they are metaphors disguised as measurement.

In our lives as citizens and consumers, we are far less reluctant to make judgments. When we choose a car, we may calculate the amount of baggage space we need, the future cost of fuel, our projected annual mileage, our disposable income; but crucially, and often critically, we also respond to style, design, personality and how they contribute to our own self-image: immeasurable factors, every one of them. Perhaps the most important decision we ever make is who we marry; but only if we prudently elect to marry for money does any element of quantification enter into our decision-making process.

The way we choose brands baffles many commentators. The whole of Naomi Klein's bestselling book *No Logo* is predicated on the assumption that brands are imposed on people by the brand owners. The first paragraph of her first chapter reads: "The astronomical growth in the wealth and cultural influence of multinational corporations over the last 15 years can arguably be traced back to a single, seemingly innocuous idea developed by management theorists in the mid-1980s: that successful corporations must primarily produce brands, as opposed to products." (That "seemingly innocuous" is a nice touch.)

But you can't, of course, produce a successful brand without producing a good product first. And a successful brand, of course, exists because people want it to exist. People differentiate between objects, people, animals instinctively and voluntarily – and rarely on a totally rational basis. People invented brand values in their

own heads centuries before the first management
theorist dared to try and classify them. Entities
that can't be said to market themselves in
any conventional sense are perceived by
their supporters and detractors to have clear
brand characteristics: newspapers, political
parties, football teams, schools and
universities.

The human brain performs an astonishing
act of computing when it does something as
apparently simple as choosing a brand of petfood.
It takes into account the quantifiable: price,
availability, pack size, ingredient list; and the
totally immeasurable: style, character, familiarity and
a wild projection of the animal's personality. When
making brand choices, the human brain has no
trouble at all in reconciling the measurable and
the immeasurable, the rational and the irrational,
quantity and quality. It understands that even
price is not a simple matter of low = good,
high = bad.

To the despair of rationalists, a high price may be seen as evidence of greater quality and therefore greater worth.

(When that very same brain is invited to explain to a researcher the reason for its choice, it should come as no surprise that the brain will favour the rational over the irrational, the quantifiable over the emotional. As we've noted before, numbers, with their beguiling precision, provide a much more respectable justification for behaviour than woolly old subjective affection.)

It may be doing her an injustice, but there seems to be a distinct note of disappointment in Naomi Klein's voice when she recounts the events of Marlboro Friday and its aftermath. According to Klein, the decision of Philip Morris to cut the price of its brand by 20% sent the pundits nuts – "announcing in frenzied unison that not only was Marlboro dead, all brand names were dead."

Surely the day of the brand – of all brands – was
over? Surely "the whole concept of branding had
lost its currency"? "Study after study showed that
baby boomers, blind to the alluring images of
advertising and deaf to the empty promises of
celebrity spokespersons, were breaking their
lifelong brand loyalties and choosing to feed
their families with private-label brands from the
supermarket." After all, she reminds us, "Marlboro
had always sold itself on the strength of its iconic
image marketing, not on anything so prosaic as its
price."

In fact, as it happened, not all the pundits were
in unison. The saner ones knew perfectly well
what consumers have always known: that value
and price are not synonymous; that value is an
individual and subjective equation, of which price
is only part; and if price is perceived to outweigh
desirability, then any sense of value goes into steep
decline.

Even in times of recession, when the concept of value is most likely to tilt in favour of the rational, it is hard to find examples, in any developed market, where the brand leader by volume is also the cheapest.

Marlboro quite simply modified its recipe of appeals; and today prospers.

So we are faced with a bit of a conundrum. In our private lives as real people, choosing things and getting married and deciding which vacation to take, we confidently embrace both the functional and the emotional; that which we can measure and that which we can't.

But when we come to business – to the business of making money (quantifiable), gaining brand share (quantifiable), building margins (quantifiable), maximising shareholder value (quantifiable) – we seem to lose our nerve a bit.

The Clipboard and the Copywriter

As long ago as 1965, David Ogilvy wrote: "The majority of businessmen are incapable of original thought because they are unable to escape from the tyranny of reason." Yet these same people, in their personal lives, shuck off the tyranny of reason on a daily basis.

In other words, it seems that those who buy brands have a more instinctive sense of worth and value than those who provide them: even when they're the same people.

The reason, of course, is the inevitable business need to argue a case, to gain support, to attract investment from a finite source. We reach, because we have to, for numbers. And we really do have to. Imagine a business plan which read in full: "When I look at this design, my heart fills with wonder and my soul soars. Please grant me $2 billion to build a prototype."

For WPP, for its companies and its competitors, numbers are just as necessary: yet their product –

that which clients buy – is more often than not unquantifiable.

A thirty-second commercial may take two hours and twenty-three minutes to write; or three weeks; or half-an-hour. But there will be no correlation between its time of incubation and its value to client.

Nor, indeed, is it possible to put a tape measure on that value to client: either before its exposure or – with any precise certainty – even afterwards.

While it is true that some disciplines find it easier than others to put a reassuring figure on return on investment – direct marketing, for example, may find it easier than public relations – it is in the nature of marketing communications that they will, infuriatingly, remain activities requiring a departure from pure rationality to invent and the application of judgment and subjective instinct to approve and support.

The reason is simple. In the recipe of appeals that any brand offers, the rational ingredients will by and large come from the core product itself: from its performance, its price, its distribution. They will be invented and selected by a rational process. In contrast, the emotional ingredients will by and large come from its communications: its messages, its look, its design, its voice. And the invention of each of these demands, at least in part, an excursion into irrationality; into inspiration and creativity; into a field of fantasy where numbers have no place. Were it to be otherwise, they would fail in their appointed task to transform that core product into an object of even greater value to its users.

There is probably no other area of business life that makes such personal demands on business people as the purchase and evaluation of a brand's communications. Deprived of both measurement and precedent (if it's been done before it's probably no good), struggling to find words to describe the non-verbal, buffeted by the winds of passionate advocacy and vehement condemnation, only judgment serves.

We may long for the comfort of the clipboard; but we need the copywriter more.

Posh Spice
& Persil

Both big brands; both alive;
and both belonging to the public

> "*Right from the beginning,*
> *I said I wanted to be more*
> *famous than Persil*
> *Automatic.*"
> **Victoria Beckham, *Learning to Fly*,**
> **The Autobiography, 2001**

I n his British Brands Group inaugural lecture last year, Tim Ambler of the London Business School set a depressingly high standard.

He raised a number of critical questions about the nature and value of brands and answered many of them. He left us with one perplexity.

If brands are as important as they are to business –
and he left us in absolutely no doubt that they are
all-important – why do chief executive officers
and their boards devote such a curiously small
proportion of their time to their health and
nourishment?

With seemly diffidence, I'd like to put forward a
possible explanation.

And as a sort of hors-d'oeuvre I offer you these 13
deeply disturbing brand facts.

• Products are made and owned by companies.
  Brands, on the other hand, are made and owned
  by people . . . by the public . . . by consumers.
• A brand image belongs not to a brand – but to
  those who have knowledge of that brand.
• The image of a brand is a subjective thing. No two
  people, however similar, hold precisely the same
  view of the same brand.

64

- That highest of all ambitions for many CEOs, a global brand, is therefore a contradiction in terms and an impossibility.

- People come to conclusions about brands as a result of an uncountable number of different stimuli: many of which are way outside the control or even influence of the product's owner.

- Brands – unlike products – are living, organic entities: they change, however imperceptibly, every single day.

- Much of what influences the value of a brand lies in the hands of its competitors.

- The only way to begin to understand the nature of brands is to strive to acquire a facility which only the greatest of novelists possess and which is so rare that it has no name.

- The study of brands – in itself a relatively recent discipline – has generated a level of jargon that not only prompts deserved derision amongst financial directors but also provides some of the most entertaining submissions to Pseuds' Corner.

• It is universally accepted that brands are a
company's most valuable asset; yet there is no
universally accepted method of measuring that
value.

• The only time you can be sure of the value of your
brand is just after you've sold it.

• It is becoming more and more apparent that, far
from brands being hierarchically inferior to
companies, only if companies are managed as
brands can they hope to be successful.

• And as if all this were not enough, in one of the
most important works about brands published
this year, the author says this: "Above all, I
found I had to accept that effective brand
communication . . . involves processes which are
uncontrolled, disordered, abstract, intuitive . . . and
frequently impossible to explain other than with
the benefit of hindsight."

All of the above, I believe to be fact. For the sake of
economy, and to some extent for effect, I have made
some half truths into whole truths and presented

them more starkly than perhaps a more
conscientious lecturer would have ventured to
do.

But all of the above statements are more or less
true.

So, in answer to Tim Ambler's implied puzzle –
why do CEOs devote so little of their time and
intelligence to the care of their most important
asset? – I advance this explanation:

Brands are fiendishly complicated, elusive, slippery,
half-real/half-virtual things. When CEOs try to
think about brands, their brains hurt.

And I sympathise. Given the nature of brands –
and the persistent perversity of consumers – who
wouldn't choose to concentrate executive time on
simple, rational, quantifiable things: like gross
margins and case rates and return on capital
invested?

I believe it to be an increasing human instinct – and an entirely understandable if highly dangerous one – to overvalue that which we can measure and to undervalue that which we can't. There is a comfort to be found in figures: they give us a sense of certainty, however false, in an otherwise chaotic world.

In his usefully corrective book *The Tyranny of Numbers*, David Boyle quotes the economist Robert Chambers:

"Quantification brings credibility. But figures and tables can deceive, and numbers construct their own realities. What can be measured and manipulated statistically is then not only seen as real; it comes to be seen as the only or the whole reality." And Chambers summed it all up like this:

"Economists have come to feel
What can't be measured isn't real.

The truth is always an amount –
Count numbers; only numbers count."

Perhaps the time will come when the mysteries of
brands will be no more; when everything about
them can be measured, valued, predicted and
replicated. Perhaps. But not in my lifetime; nor
even, I think, in yours.

So, with the hors-d'oeuvre behind us, my aim from
now on will be to explore most of those 13 deeply
inconvenient brand facts rather more thoroughly:
not to provide answers or solutions but more, I
hope, to shine a little light on these murky matters.
Thinking about brands should be a productive
rather than a painful occupation – and should lead
to a greater confidence in taking intuitive decisions.
More often than not, such decisions turn out to be
gratifyingly simple.

First, my thanks to Victoria Beckham for the title of
this lecture.

If her early ambition to be more famous than Persil
Automatic seemed to you surprising – or even
laughable – it shouldn't have done. It was very
astute of the young Posh Spice to choose not
Robbie Williams nor Sir Cliff Richard nor
Madonna as her benchmark of fame but the
country's best-known washing powder.

Because just about the only thing that successful
brands have in common is a kind of fame. Indeed,
it's been suggested that brands are the real
celebrities. And for most human beings, fame not
only holds a powerful fascination but bestows an
incalculable value on anything that enjoys it. We
value the famous far more highly than the little
known.

I do not think, as is often suggested, that this is a
new phenomenon. Nor do I think, another social
theory, that we the public have invented celebrities
as a replacement for the vanished aristocracy. Rather,
I think that the aristocracy were of interest to us

peasants not because they were aristocratic but because they were the most famous people around. We should not assume that everyone who stands in the rain to catch a glimpse of Her Majesty the Queen is a royalist. The Royal Family continue to engage the interest of us peasants at least as much because they are celebrities as because they are royal.

And then, as Andy Warhol so memorably observed, with the arrival of mass media, particularly of course television, fame became technically available to everyone: if only for 15 minutes.

It is one of the peculiarities of fame – whether for people or products – that real fame appears to be spectacularly untargeted. By that I mean, that the most famous people in the world are known to an infinitely greater number of people than their particular talent or profession would seem either to demand or to deserve.

Victoria Beckham is one such example. So is Madonna. Real fame implies being known to millions of people who have never bought your records and never will. Stephen Hawking is known to millions of people who will never understand a word he writes; and to 10 times as many who will never even try to.

To the consternation of media planners and buyers in advertising agencies, the same is true for brands. A brand, if it is to enjoy genuine celebrity, must be known to a circle of people that far exceeds what we in the business so chillingly call its target group.

It is not enough for BMW to be known only to that 5% of the population wealthy enough even to contemplate buying one. For BMW to enjoy real fame, it needs to be known almost indiscriminately.

I do not know why this should be; I only know that it is.

There are those who believe that it's all to do with envy and one-upmanship: what's the point of your driving about in a £50,000 BMW if 95 per cent of us peasants don't realise just how successful you must be to own one? There may be a bit of truth in this theory: but it surely can't explain the value that Persil derives from being universally famous? And doesn't it seem improbable that we pop a six-pack of Coke or a packet of Oxo cubes into our shopping basket in the hope of arousing envy and admiration in the hearts of all the others at the checkout counter?

There are thousands of great and public brands that virtually no one is debarred from buying on the grounds of price – yet they possess a value that lesser-known products lack.

For manufacturers, for brand marketers, I don't think the question of why matters very much. It only matters that it is. Fame is the fundamental value that strong brands own.

You do, of course, have to be famous for something: and we come to that later.

The matter of fame takes us naturally to the matter of brand ownership.

Of course, in a legal sense, the company owns the brand. But for a company to *feel* that it owns its brands is to tempt it to believe that it has total control over them: and it does not.

Forget the marketing-speak. The image of a brand is no more nor less than the result of its fame: its reputation. And like a reputation, it can be found in only one place: in the minds of people.

Lord Archer, Sir Richard Branson, Victoria Beckham, Rudolph Giuliani, Harry Potter and the Prince of Wales are all public figures; and like all public figures, they have reputations. But you will not find these reputations neatly defined and filed away in Companies' House, nor lodged with their respective solicitors. The only way you will find a reputation is by opening up other people's minds and peering inside. The same is true for the image of the brand.

Nor, of course, does a public figure have a single, constant reputation, shared by everyone. One of the most potent political reputations over the last 30 years has been that of Mrs Thatcher. Not only has that reputation changed dramatically over time, but it has never been remotely homogenous.

This very same person, *indisputably* the same person, at exactly the same point in time, has been seen as both tyrant and liberator: and a thousand variations in between.

Her views, actions and achievements have been known to everyone. The stimuli have been common. But the response to those stimuli has been as varied as the characters of those who have known of her existence. Mrs Thatcher's reputation does not belong to Mrs Thatcher; it belongs to the 50-odd million people in Britain who know of her existence – and many more abroad – and it comes in as many different shades.

Tiresome though it may be to accept, the same is true for brands. The most valuable part of a brand . . . the added value bit . . . the bit that protects respectable margins and fills up the reservoir of future cash flow . . . the bit that distinguishes a brand from a mere product . . . *doesn't belong to it*. It belongs to its public. And for those who are loyal to brands, this sense of ownership, of possession, is strong and often overtly recognised. It's 30 years or so since I first heard real people in group discussions talking openly and quite unselfconsciously about their favourite washing powder. But they didn't just talk about Persil: they talked about *my* Persil.

So the image of the brand – its brand reputation – that which makes it the shareholders' most valuable asset – doesn't belong to it. It belongs to all those who give thought to it.

No wonder CEOs prefer to spend their time counting things.

But the fact that the image of the brand doesn't reside with the brand is not quite such a depressing truth as it may seem. Because it leads us to wonder how exactly these images . . . these brand reputations . . . are formed in the first place.

Many marketing companies, and even more of their marketing advisors, pride themselves on their ability to build brands. But of course neither group builds brands: because brands are built in people's heads.

What the most skilful of marketing companies do, with great sensitivity and unceasing vigilance, is provide some of the raw material from which brands are built. There is an enormous difference.

Many years ago, I wrote that people build brands as birds build nests, from scraps and straws we chance upon. The metaphor remains a useful one – but it needs to be both modified and amplified.

I said earlier, as one of my 13 unpalatable brand facts, that "people come to conclusions about brands as a result of an uncountable number of different stimuli."

That's true – but we can count some of them. These are some of the scraps and straws from which people build brands.

Let me start with the *product*. It's often said that a brand is a product with added communication: but it seems to me that the intrinsic product – its delivery, its function – must itself be the primary brand communication. No washing powder which fails to deliver high standards of detergency will survive – however skilfully marketed. No beer that fails to please the taste buds – however great its advertising budget – will survive. Function is the first and permanent requirement for brand success. I shall talk much in this lecture about brand reputation and added value: but let me first echo a warning issued earlier this year by Niall FitzGerald in his *Marketing Society* annual lecture.

He identified the manufacturer who starts out by being technologically very advanced – and is deservedly very successful. As his market gets more and more competitive, he comes to realise that he needs both product performance *and* brand character in order to stay ahead. Brilliantly, an image is built for his brand – so that users not only respect it but feel loyal to it as well. He is even more successful.

Then comes the critical stage. He becomes such an enthusiast for the notion of brand personality – and falls so deeply in love with his own – that he comes to believe that competitive product performance is no longer his highest priority. So he neglects to innovate, he neglects to invest in R&D, he stops listening intently for those first faint murmurs of discontent – and, for a month or two, or even a year or two – his success continues and his profits mount.

And then, with savage suddenness, his once healthy brand becomes an invalid: losing share and reputation with precipitate speed.

Because when people discover what's been done, that a once-loved brand has taken its users for granted, those users will be totally and brutally unforgiving. And their desertion will have something of vengeance about it.

I shan't talk much more about function: not because it's of little importance but because it's so self-evidently central to brand success that reiteration of that truth should be unnecessary.

The next most obvious clue to brand character
is advertising: often claimed to be the greatest
brand builder of them all. I spent over 30 years in
advertising; but unless you define advertising in
an unusually liberal way, I wouldn't necessarily
support that claim. That there has to be some
communication between a brand and its public is
obvious; but its name, its packaging, its stores if it
has any, its vans, its news value can all give people
important clues to a brand's character: and in some
instances, these non-advertising communications
media will be the all-important ones. Today, we are
principally concerned with manufacturers' brands,
offered for sale in a competitive market place.
But let's not forget the great schools, the great
newspapers, the great football clubs: all of
which not only perfectly fit the definition of
brands but help us understand their nature.
In few if any instances do brands of this kind
owe their power and influence primarily to
advertising.

Then *price*. Price is a wonderfully deceptive item. "Look at me," says price: "I'm a number. So you can compare me to the prices of all my competitors and find out which is best." For a second or two, would-be rational man may feel a surge of hope: at last, the comforting feel of ground beneath the feet.

But of course, as everybody knows, price offers no such universal reassurance. Price is both an objective fact and a stimulus likely to elicit any number of very different subjective responses. The same low price can simultaneously lower the barrier to entry and increase suspicions about quality.

It is only commentators who confuse price with value for money; consumers never do.

Consumers know that value-for-money is a calculation that they make, as individuals, often intuitively; and that price is just one factor within that calculation. Like the image of a brand, and for the same reason, value for money is an individual

82

concept, individually arrived at – however widely shared it may turn out to be.

From time to time I try to identify a significant consumer market sector – detergents, toilet tissue, beans, packaged cakes, confectionery, cigarettes, canned beer – where the brand with the lowest price is also the market leader. In countries where choice is still a distant concept, there are of course many such examples. But in our more fortunate world, accustomed as we've been for 50 years or more now to a range of options in everything we buy, I can still think of none.

And this is not, as the rationalists would have us believe, because the gullible masses are lured into paying for some intangible image; it's because the masses are made up of individuals, each of whom is perfectly capable of determining which price demanded most accurately matches which set of satisfactions delivered: not universally, of course – but for himself or herself.

One of the many functions of price is famously encapsulated, and with great marketplace success, by Stella Artois: "Reassuringly expensive."

Promotions are almost as deceptive a stimulus as price and for much the same reason. Surely a two-for-the-price-of-one, a banded offer of that new CD, the chance of a free holiday in the Caribbean: surely such bargains must lead to more sales and therefore be good for the brand?

Maybe the first; but not necessarily the second.

People – in which I continue to include you and me: not some remote and alien consuming body – people interpret all brand clues with instinctive intelligence.

Marketing people give a great deal of thought to what people think of brands. What brands appear to think of people is at least as interesting.

When brands make clear and often impertinent assumptions about us, we notice. When I get yet another invitation to apply for a platinum credit card, I know exactly the assumption that this brand has made about me. It has assumed that I will enjoy flashing a platinum card in front of headwaiters; that I will appreciate an automatic if expensive overdraft facility of £10,000; that I drive a car with a personalised number plate and wear open-backed driving gloves while doing so. I resent these assumptions deeply. And I would, of course, resent them at least as deeply if they were absolutely accurate.

Most promotions fall neatly into one of two categories: bribes or bonuses.

The bonus makes this assumption about me: that I will appreciate some token of gratitude for my continued custom.

The bribe makes this assumption about me: that I will buy something I never wanted in the first place because it's now cheaper.

The first congratulates and flatters me; the second insults me.

The signal that the bonus sends out is one of generosity and confidence; the bonus enhances the brand. The signal that the bribe sends out is one of insecurity and desperation; the bribe diminishes the brand.

So the promotion – the offer – is more than a short-term sales incentive. It's another clue to brand character: one of those many scraps and straws from which people build brands inside their heads.

Advertising, packaging, price and promotions have this in common: they are all within the control of the marketing company. To be rather more accurate: the transmission of these brand stimuli is within the control of the marketing company. Their *reception*, however, is not.

Among all my deeply disturbing brand facts, this is the one most calculated to cause distracted CEOs sleepless nights – which is probably why they choose not to think about it.

I said at the start: "The only way to begin to understand the nature of brands is to strive to acquire a facility which only the greatest of novelists possess and which is so rare that it has no name." The last part of that sentence is not quite true.

In her 1996 Reith Lecture, Jean Aitchison wrote: "An effective persuader must be able to imagine events from another person's point of view. In fashionable jargon, he or she must have 'A Theory of Mind'."

A Theory of Mind may be fashionable jargon among academics and psychiatrists but it's far from fashionable anywhere else; nor does it deserve to be. It is a hopelessly inadequate term for a rare and priceless facility. And 'empathy' is in its own way worse, since we think we know what it means but don't.

The ability "to imagine events from another person's point of view . . ." to see things through other people's eyes . . . to put oneself in someone else's shoes: it might be a more respected skill were it only to have a decent name.

I've been brooding about this rare ability for a very long time. When I was about seven years old, I was taken to have tea with the only rich relation we had. As we were about to leave, she reached for her purse, took out five one pound notes and gave them to me.

I was, at the time, on two shillings a week pocket money. What I held in my hand was one year's gross income.

Then she peered at the notes and said, "Oh dear. Those two are *very* dirty. I couldn't possibly let you go away with notes like that." And she took back two of the one pound notes – and didn't replace them.

My aunt did not possess a complete understanding of The Theory of Mind. There was no meanness in her action; only a kind of blindness. She saw those two notes through her eyes only.

We were both looking at the same notes. They had a measured, agreed, universally accepted worth: they were worth one pound each. But to me they represented riches beyond imagination and to her they were a Boxing Day tip for the milkman. There is, I believe, no commonly accepted name for this form of blindness but it is widespread – and not only in marketing.

Most of us in the rich and fortunate West are genuinely bewildered to discover that the way of life we know with such untroubled certainty to be civilised seems, with an equivalent certainty, to be the epitome of blasphemy and greed to others.

Jean Aitchison is right. The ability to imagine events from another's point of view is the first qualifying talent of the would-be effective persuader. Those scraps and straws over which we painstakingly pore have no universal significance.

Through different eyes, a single bank note can represent enough Smarties for the entire summer holidays, with a balsa wood glider thrown in; or a handy wedge to stop the table wobbling.

The poor old focus group has had a thoroughly hostile press in recent years – unfairly, I believe. And the reason for that hostility is a confusion in the minds of many commentators between the knowledge you gain from a focus group – and the use you put that knowledge to.

If focus groups tell you that the single European currency is regarded with deep hostility but that corporal punishment has acquired a new popularity, you will deserve every bit of odium hurled at you if, with absolutely no further thought, you pull out of Europe and bring back the birch.

But it is irresponsible government – and potentially suicidal management – deliberately to stay ignorant of the content of other people's minds.

You do not have to agree with what you discover. You should certainly not expect people to tell you what to do next. Nor should you be surprised if what people say they want turns out to be very different from what they subsequently choose. But you should never find yourself ambushed.

I cannot believe that Marks & Spencer was anything other than astonished by the severity of their fall from grace; yet neither can I believe that the signs weren't there for years before it happened.

Marks & Spencer has competitors: and the tiresome thing about competitors, other than their very existence, is that what *they* do has a significant effect on your own reputation.

We all have invisible maps in our heads, on which we plot the position of competing brands. Every brand is allocated its own, unique space. There may or may not be such things as parity products; there are certainly no parity brands.

Fifteen years ago, our mental map of the daily broadsheet newspaper market in this country would have allocated clear positions for *The Daily Telegraph*, *The Guardian* and *The Times*. And then *The Independent* was launched with considerable effect, and all the existing co-ordinates subtly changed: because reputations, as well as being subjective, are also relative. A brand is defined in our minds at least as much by its competitors as by its own behaviour.

These changes to brands take place all the time. A new competitor may occasion a perceptible change – but the really dangerous changes are the daily, tiny, immeasurable, imperceptible changes that accumulate invisibly over time until they've gained often unstoppable significance.

It is all this that leads me to say that brands are living, organic things – because all the time, those with knowledge of a brand are changing. They may grow richer or poorer and will certainly grow older; and as the perceiver changes, so inevitably, does the perception. If a marketing company closes both its eyes and its ears; if it relies on the single dimension of current sales; if it believes that yesterday's successful strategy is an infallible guide to tomorrow's profit: then it's heading for disillusionment of barometric severity.

A commitment to monitoring changes in brand perception demands constant vigilance – and an unusual degree of corporate humility. But it's an absolutely essential procedure for all brand stewards anxious to protect themselves from extremely unwelcome surprises.

The means by which these scraps and straws infiltrate the human mind remain something of a mystery.

The advertising world, in the teeth of instinct and much evidence, insisted for years that brand choice was the result of persuasive argument consciously processed.

Consumers were assumed to notice an advertisement; become engaged by its overt promise or proposition; and be thereby consciously persuaded to buy. It was a neat, linear, deterministic model that brought great comfort to disorientated advertisers and communications researchers alike: it offered consistency, rationality and some deeply desirable opportunities for measurement. The model put much emphasis on both attention and memory: and, what luck, both could be readily quantified.

It was always a deeply unsatisfactory model and, in practice, was widely ignored by advertising practitioners. But despite the occasional guerrilla attack on its underlying premise, it remained the least worst respectable model in town.

This year, Robert Heath has published an important monograph: I quoted from it earlier. It's called *The Hidden Power of Advertising* but its subtitle is a much more accurate label: *How low involvement processing influences the way we choose brands.*

I will not attempt to take you through his own processes of thought; it is enough for you to know that it's a rigorous work and draws on new understanding from the worlds of neuroscience and psychology. But I will quote at some length from his own summary.

"Consumers in general regard most reputable brands as performing similarly and because of this they do not regard learning about brands as being very important. Brand decisions tend to be made intuitively rather than rationally.

"Because it is not seen as very important, most brand information tends not so much to be actively 'sought' as passively 'acquired'. Brand communication, such as advertising, tends to be processed at very low attention levels and we generally do not work very hard to learn or understand what we are being told about the brand.

"Mostly we process brand communication using an automatic mental process called low involvement processing. Low involvement processing is a complex mixture of semiconscious and subconscious activity. Much of it involves what is known as 'implicit' learning – learning that takes place without you knowing that you are learning.

"The way our long-term memory works means that the more often something is processed alongside a brand, the more permanently it becomes associated with that brand. Thus, it is the perceptions and simple concepts, repeatedly and 'implicitly' reinforced at low levels of attention, which tend over time to define brands in our minds. And because implicit memory is more durable than explicit memory, these brand associations, once learned, are rarely forgotten."

To me, that makes absolute sense. It feels right.

When I examine the inside of my own head, and look at some of the brand reputations that reside there, I cannot for the life of me trace their source.

I have learnt without knowing I was learning; I have absorbed, by some unconscious osmotic process, a range of stimuli – and from these, equally unconsciously, I have constructed a coherent brand character.

So let me return to these scraps and straws from which we, as individuals, infer so much.

And let me move from those brand communications over which the marketing company has theoretical control – product, advertising, packaging, price, promotions, for example – to brand encounters of a far more accidental nature.

You see a truck, boldly branded, driving badly on the M25. You see a pack in the house of someone you dislike. You read that the company that makes the product has been taken to court for racial discrimination. The daughter of a friend is fired by the parent company. You receive an illiterate and ill-spelt letter from head office. After holding on for 25 minutes, you have still to speak to a human being at the company's call centre.

Like people, brands have body language; and it's a language we understand. Every time we encounter a brand, we make an infinitesimal and subconscious adjustment to our personally constructed brand picture: and in each of the instances mentioned above, those adjustments will not be in the brand's favour.

And the reason it matters is this. The luxury of choice that we all enjoy; the fact that, however crassly sometimes, competitive companies are fighting for our cash and our custom; all this means that, in allocating our loyalty, we welcome reasons to reject a brand almost as eagerly as reasons to prefer it.

As Professor Ehrenberg and others have long demonstrated, and as Robert Heath reminds us, what is called brand loyalty is very rarely a truly exclusive matter. We assume all alternatives to be broadly acceptable; we all have favoured repertoires within each brand category; and we all want to make brand decisions with a minimum of anguish. So however infinitesimally negative a brand encounter may be, the damage it may do to that brand's competitive standing may be serious.

The way we interpret the body language of brands means that the apparently trivial can be greatly significant.

In the performing arts, or so I'm told, they preach something called 'transitive action'. And what this means, or so I'm told, is that good writers and directors encourage an audience to deduce character and motivation not from what is explicitly said but from what that audience observes being *done*.

The best brand stewards, too, encourage their potential customers to deduce character not just from claim and assertion – from presentation – but from transitive action: from brand behaviour.

I have long admired a supermarket in the States. Proud of their reputation for fresh produce, they had always removed the outside leaves of lettuces before putting them on display. One day, a lowly member of staff made a modest suggestion: and from then on, those outside leaves, instead of being consigned to the garbage bin, were popped into plastic bags and given away free at the checkout – to families whose children kept pet rabbits. Naturally, they called them BunnyBags. I don't think it absurd to suggest that, as a result, 15 years on, those children will choose to take their own children to that very same supermarket.

Some years ago, a friend of mine was a lunch guest in the Connaught Hotel dining room – and noticed his host first of all patting his pockets ineffectively and then peering miserably at the menu. No word was said: but within a minute, a waiter had appeared with a velvet-lined tray on which were displayed ten pairs of reading glasses of different levels of magnification. My friend, the guest, has been a loyal Connaught user ever since; and remember – it wasn't even him who needed the glasses.

BunnyBags and reading specs: two very small examples of brand behaviour with much in common.

Both showed an understanding of A Theory of Mind: they put themselves in the place of their customers; they understood what it was like to be a small child with pet rabbits or an embarrassed businessman finding small print difficult.

Both understood the importance of transitive action, of brand body language. They invited their customers to infer, from behaviour, rather than to accept from boastful claim or assertion.

And both realised – or simply, perhaps, instinctively felt – that the apparently trivial can, in interpretation, take on quite disproportionate and positive significance.

I believe the best brand stewards of the future will recognise the potential power of such body language; and demand much more in the way of brand action and rather less in the way of empty self-praise.

They will also, I believe, have to come to terms with perhaps the most daunting of my propositions.

There was once a time when most brands had no publicly recognised parents. You bought your packet of Persil or your jar of Marmite and knew absolutely nothing, and cared rather less, about the company behind them. For two quite different but converging sets of reasons, that is changing fast – and will continue to do so.

The age of the free-standing brand is nearly over. For reasons widely understood, most brands now – and nearly all new brands – trumpet the name of their parent. The parent may be a company or an already established brand but the reasoning is the same: let's leverage our brand equity; let's trade

on the trust we've already so painstakingly and
expensively built.

But of course, just as the good news can be shared
and spread through such linkages, so can the bad.
Free-standing brands – orphan brands, with no
known parents – may be non-contagious. But when
brand relationships are not just public but widely
publicised, bad news from one can rapidly
become an epidemic.

The effect of the internet is to accelerate the chances
of brand contagion. The internet means that there is
nowhere to hide. You cannot charge $350 for a pair
of chinos and pay third world workers $3.50 a day
to make them and hope to go unnoticed. You
cannot deprive your own workforce of knowledge of
your company's performance when they have ready
access to it elsewhere. You cannot ignore the
conversations that your networked employees are
having with your networked customers. For more
on this, consult the *The Cluetrain Manifesto*: a

splendidly anarchic rant, of internet origins. Once you have read it, feel free to ignore quite a lot of it; but don't fail to read it and don't ignore it all.

And – as Tim Ambler pointed out – Naomi Klein's book *No Logo* is not, as is widely supposed, an attack on brands; it's an exposé, as she sees it, of the double standards of multinational corporations and the risks they run.

This convergence of company and brand, this reckless openness of communication, this threat to general reputation that any specific transgression now poses, is quite enough reason for the chief executive to take a very close interest indeed in the management of his brands. Or perhaps I should say, his brand.

But there's another, more positive reason.

Today, to a marked extent, all brands are service brands. Other than street traders, few businesses now see their only function as being simply to make a sale. After-sales service, relationship marketing, the concept of lifetime value, the growth of interactive media: all these trends and developments mean that the creation and maintenance of a valued brand should now quite clearly be the responsibility not of some relatively lowly brand manager but of the chief executive of the enterprise itself.

This is not just a defensive measure: the competitive opportunities presented by the deliberate creation of a corporate brand are immense. They are described in detail, with impressive case studies, in a book called *The Masterbrand Mandate* by Lynn Upshaw and Earl Taylor.

The extension of the principles of branding from product to company means opening up the whole marketing strategy to absolutely everyone within that company. It means recognising that every corporate action, every corporate decision, every corporate communication will be seen as a clue – as

one of those all-important scraps and straws from
which people build brands.

It means confiding in your workforce and training
them and asking them for constructive suggestions.
It means trusting them to respond to customer
dissatisfaction both immediately and personally,
without cowering behind head office instructions.
It means as conscious an application of internal
marketing – internal communications – as we give to
our external marketing.

If you want to get a feel for the corporate brand,
think of some successful first generation companies –
companies such as Dyson or Pret à Manger. Still
led by their forceful founders, they embody and
broadcast a single-minded and unifying set of values.
And that which is done instinctively and obsessively
by such pioneers can be done equally well by the
chief executives of long established companies: but
only if they are prepared first to understand and
then to undertake the role of brand steward.

The value to the company, of course, if they get it right, extends well beyond sales levels and profit margins: it extends into labour relations and press relations and investor relations; it helps in the retention of valued executives; it gives them a competitive edge when recruiting new graduates.

But while recognising and recommending the masterbrand strategy, let me return to the Niall FitzGerald warning.

However brilliantly reputation management may be masterminded, and however much that reputation contributes to differentiation and competitive success, if there's anything fundamentally wrong with the product, then ultimate failure – I'm extremely happy to report – remains inevitable.

The authors of *The Masterbrand Mandate* devote a whole page of praise to a giant American company which was "transforming itself into a brand-based organisation." They report that "Messages about creativity and innovation are sent to employees through their intranet, via T-shirts, in print and television advertising, at employee meetings, in self-training programs." This is the corporation that won *Fortune* magazine's "Most Innovative US Company" award four times in the mid-1990s – and it's called Enron.

It's stories like this that give immense comfort to brand averse CEOs. "There you are," they say, "it's all smoke and mirrors stuff. Only charlatans rabbit on about brands. All puff and no substance. Never lasts. Now let's get back to counting things."

But of course, the authors weren't wrong to recognise what Enron was doing. If the fundamentals of the Enron operation had been solid, what Enron was doing would have indeed been admirable. An obsession with the management of brands must never be at the expense of functional efficiency. Indeed, as I hope I've stressed, and stressed indelibly, functional efficiency is a strong brand's first prerequisite. But that simple thought seems to get forever lost.

Benjamin Franklin
and the
Kuala Lumpur Question

The city of Florence recently announced the winner of a competition, open to architects throughout the world, for the design of a new railway station. As is the custom in these cases, all the short-listed designs are now on public display, including that of the winner, Norman Foster.

Even to an untutored eye, the time, thought, money, passion, talent and love lavished on every one of them is painfully apparent. To study their brilliant fusion of function and form is to feel a huge sense of sympathy – not just for the losers but also for the members of the adjudicating panel whose job it was to make the final choice. There were to be no consolation prizes. There could be only one winner.

How in the name of justice was that single winner to be chosen and the rest confined to oblivion?

I don't, of course, know; but I'm entirely confident that the process can only have been completed by that which in certain advertising circles is known as the Kuala Lumpur Question*.

To understand the implications of the Kuala Lumpur Question, you must first put yourself in the place of any adjudicator faced with the need, as were the Florentine panellists, to make a single choice from multiple offerings, many of which are excellent.

Let us say that you have in front of you 150 written applications for a single job vacancy and that you must first reduce that number to 10; and later, from that 10, choose one.

*No slight to Kuala Lumpur is intended. In Malaysia, the Kuala Lumpur Question might well be the Tierra del Fuego Question.

112

Benjamin Franklin and the Kuala Lumpur Question

You may start by believing that you will scan through those applications and select only the most promising: that you will search for the positive. But very quickly indeed, if you're at all self-aware, you'll notice that a subtle change has come over your assessment process. Rather than taking out your hi-liter pen and emphasising the most appealing characteristics of the most promising applicants, you begin to look for errors and omissions. Rather than looking for reasons for inclusion, your eyes will begin to scan the papers for evidence to justify rejection. You find yourself longing to alight on the small false fact, the typographical error, the relatively unimpressive qualification, the failure to do the most basic homework about your own company. You seize on these often insignificant features with relief and gratitude: with a clear conscience, you may now begin to eliminate; your candidate pile is already down to 149, 148, 147, 146 . . .

The Objective Disqualifier

Advertising agencies, brand consultants and professional advisers of all kinds routinely find themselves taking part in beauty parades, presenting their credentials to potential clients in competition with many others. Understandably, they concentrate on their proprietary skills and their authenticated achievements; so they are not always ready for the Kuala Lumpur Question.

"Tell me," says the potential client, now half way through the fifth impressive presentation, "Do you have an office in Kuala Lumpur?"

It is possible, I suppose, that access to an office in Kuala Lumpur is indeed of cardinal commercial importance to this client. It is very much more likely, however, that the client is searching with something approaching desperation for an apparently respectable reason for the elimination of at least one of the candidate agencies. However trivial it may be, he needs an Objective Disqualifier.

On receiving the verdict a week or two later, the candidate agency in question reacts with disbelief and outrage. "They loved the work we do for X, they thought our strategy was fantastic, they found the chemistry between us sensational – yet they've bumped us off the bloody list *because we haven't got an office in Kuala Lumpur!*"

The outrage is understandable but the disbelief is naïve. This process of selection, or something very close to it, is inevitable in any competitive situation where there are more high quality applicants than opportunities. The luckless Florentine adjudicators, faced with a great many brilliantly conceived designs for railway stations, must, towards the end of the process, have scrutinised each meticulously made-to-scale model not for evidence of perfection but for evidence of imperfection.

The truth of all this may have been apparent enough to competitive professions for a very long time. A little belatedly perhaps, marketing companies are waking up to the fact that, in consumer markets, too, there are many more applicants than opportunities; more production than consumption; more supply than demand.

As touched on very briefly in last year's WPP annual report essay, greatly increased consumer choice and confidence mean that individuals making brand selections behave more and more like the adjudicating panel of an architectural competition – and for exactly the same reasons. Faced with an array of competitive brands – all known to be functionally satisfactory (which is why they are competitive) and all pleading persuasively for our custom – we have no choice but to eliminate: so "in allocating our loyalty we welcome reasons to reject a brand almost as eagerly as reasons to prefer it." At some level of consciousness, we search for the Objective Disqualifier, however trivial.

Eliminate the negative

It's been recognised for at least 70 years that few everyday brands enjoy significant functional advantages over their competitors; and that even when they do exist, they tend to be short-lived. The growth of marketing communications over that same period owes much to their acknowledged ability to establish and maintain brands whose distinctive positioning derives at least as much from brand character as from brand performance.

In a future which promises still more over-capacity in production, fierce competition in prices, elusive margins and a consuming public increasingly asserting its democratic right to be picky, there can be little doubt that marketing communications are in for a period of sustained demand. But maybe, in this second stage of consumer enfranchisement, we now need to do rather more than accentuate the positive; however difficult it may prove to be, we'll have to learn to anticipate and eliminate the negative as well.

Conventional research won't help us very much.
What do marketing directors value most highly in
advertising agencies? The trade press regularly
conducts research on this subject, and this is what
marketing directors value: an understanding of their
business, creativity, strategic insights, good
management. Marketing directors will never confess
to a researcher that what they are really looking for is
an office in Kuala Lumpur; because, of course, they
aren't. The ownership of an office in Kuala Lumpur
will never, of itself, win you business. The absence
of one, however unjustly, may be used to justify
your losing it.

Beers, banks and candy bars

Exactly the same set of principles applies to
consumers of beers, banks or candy bars. And
exactly the same process applies not only to the
selection of an option in the first place but also to
its subsequent deselection.

What do I want from a bank? I want efficiency, accuracy, availability and security; and – sentimentalist that I am – I'd also like to believe that my bank sometimes thinks of me as a human being.

I'd once had the same bank for about 20 years and felt a general discontent about it. Yet it continued to provide efficiency, accuracy, availability and security: so I stayed with it. Then one day, very politely, I asked them why I was having the occasional problem getting my bank card accepted. Time passed – and I then got a letter from the manager expressing surprise that I had encountered such a problem since he himself was having no trouble whatsoever. And that's all he said.

Something snapped. I'd found the excuse I'd been subconsciously looking for: the Objective Disqualifier. So I fired them. And I have no doubt that they were utterly astonished that such a trivial incident could have prompted me to jettison 20 years of amiable rubbing along in order to embark on the fearful journey of moving my bank account.

There's been a great deal of talk over the last 10 years or so for the need for integrated communications. We are all agreed by now, I think, that our multitude of different brand communications needs to be carefully monitored for coherence and cohesion; that advertising, PR, direct marketing, website design and maintenance, in-store display, promotions and perhaps a dozen other consumer encounters need to complement each other; need to be integrated.

What often seems to be forgotten, however, is that all brand communications, however disparate and chaotic, inevitably end up being integrated anyway. The trouble is, they end up being integrated not by the brand's managers but by the brand's potential users. And the way that consumers conduct this integration is seldom to the benefit of the brand's reputation.

The receivers of brand communications, like all receivers, abhor dissonance. We find it impossible to think as highly of a brand in its totality if just one minor abrasive factor disturbs its polished surface. One small disrupting experience, one jarring note in its communications, one piece of brand behaviour that contradicts the brand's promise: and, in our need to find consonance, we will downgrade our ratings until everything fits again. By the time we've completed integrating its incoherent communications, the brand will be diminished in our minds.

Back to 1758
So two dangerous truths both collide and collude. In trying to make coherent sense of a brand's contradictory signals, the relatively unimportant flaw takes on a disproportionately destructive role; while at exactly the same time, in our quest to make simple, fret-free choices, to eliminate options with a clear conscience, we search for and embrace any evidence of inadequacy. We identify some minor

deficiency; then press it into service as our Objective Disqualifier.

In *Poor Richard's Almanack* for 1758, Benjamin Franklin foreshadowed all of this. He urged "circumspection and care, even in the smallest matters, because sometimes a little neglect may breed great mischief." And he reminded us:

For want of a nail, the shoe was lost; for want of a shoe, the horse was lost; for want of a horse, the rider was lost; for want of a rider, the message was lost; for want of a message, the battle was lost; for want of a battle, the kingdom was lost. And all for the want of a horseshoe nail.

In modern marketing, the horseshoe nail may be one of a thousand apparently insignificant factors. Many of those factors, organisationally, may be officially outside the province or responsibility of the marketing director. An unresponsive call centre; the failure to correct a faulty product feature; a clumsy letter from head office; a rumour on the internet; a minor change to a trusted product's formulation: to the besieged consumer actively seeking an equivalent of the Kuala Lumpur Question, subconsciously on the lookout for an Objective Disqualifier, each of these trivial occurrences may be enough to lose the brand a lifetime loyalist.

They can't all be anticipated, of course, and they can't all be prevented. But they do need to be identified and they should never take us by surprise. In a world where virtually every brand has some element of after-sales service about it, an ability to recover, apologise and make amends for the inconsequent may become as commercially necessary as the maintenance of basic product quality.

The Steak & Kidney Pie
That Wasn't

— the end is in sight for Sizzle Marketing

Just about every marketing strategy written over the last 50 years or so contains an introductory section entitled The New Challenges.

In it, the author catalogues the astonishing range of obstacles that make the achievement of that year's agreed targets uniquely difficult. The list will include: increasing competition, inflated media rates, attenuated lead-times, adverse exchange rates and – a particular favourite – the increasing sophistication of the consumer. Marketing has been getting more and more difficult for so many years now it's a miracle that we can still function at all.

And now we may expect a new hazard to join the old favourites. As convincingly demonstrated by Barry

Schwartz in his book *The Paradox of Choice*, today's affluent consumer is faced with such an over-abundance of choice that a kind of paralysis sets in. "Clinging tenaciously to all the choices available to us contributes to bad decisions, to anxiety, stress, and dissatisfaction – even to clinical depression." "Unlimited choice" may "produce genuine suffering." So here's another setback for those of us in marketing: an excess of choice leading to consumer stasis. We can only look back with envy at our fortunate, carefree predecessors who were lucky enough to be in marketing when marketing was easy.

But in this belief, of course, we delude ourselves. More often than not, that catalogue of New Challenges is trotted out as a preemptive strike against the risk of failure. There's little meaningful evidence to suggest that marketing today is any more difficult than it was 50 years ago.

When we talk so plaintively about the increasing sophistication of the consumer, what we're really referring to is a past that never existed; to those good old days when all we had to do was instruct the peasants to go out and buy something – and they, with a deferential touch of the cap, would mutely obey. And what we imply (though never openly say) is that, because these newly sophisticated consumers have seen through our strategy, it's getting harder and harder to get away with it.

This implication is curiously insulting to both consumers and marketing. Consumers, as David Ogilvy reminded the world some 40 years ago, have never been morons; and good marketing has never been about getting away with it.

What is certainly true is that we all adapt over time to changes in communications techniques. Compare the editing and dialogue of a good 1954 feature film with the editing and dialogue of a good 2004 feature film. Note the confidence and economy with which today's directors employ hints and clues; trust their audiences to fill in gaps, to understand nuances, to follow story lines. And that confidence is entirely justified: not because today's audience is a smarter audience but because they've all had more practice; they've learnt the language of filmmaking.

In just the same way, people have learnt the language of advertising and marketing; but again, this is not because they're smarter – or indeed, more sophisticated. It's not that they've seen through us; they just don't want to be subjected to old-fashioned marketing any more than they want to wear old-fashioned clothes.

And secondly, of course, these changes in our consumers' marketing literacy – their increased familiarity with marketing's techniques – have an impact not only on us. They apply, with equal force, to every one of our competitors; which makes it logically difficult to argue that the increased sophistication of our consumers presents problems exclusively confined to us. All the time, it's true, the nature of the playing field changes a bit – but it always remains level.

Elmer Wheeler's Legacy

Of all the marketing techniques that consumers are now consciously aware of, there's one we can trace back to Elmer Wheeler. It was this inspirational Depression-era salesman who first exhorted his followers to "sell the sizzle not the steak". Wheeler originally meant it as a reminder that effective salesmanship concentrates not on an exhaustive list of a product's attributes but rather on the benefits that those attributes deliver. When many years later, Theodore Levitt reminded us that people didn't want a quarter-inch drill, they wanted a quarter-inch hole, he was making the same durable point. Over time, however, Elmer's adage seems to have drifted a bit in meaning. Today, too often, it encourages marketing people to concentrate on the sizzle to the exclusion of the steak; to believe that the intrinsic quality of a product is secondary to its image. This

is dangerous stuff and people – real people – have
sniffed it out with growing disapproval.

In a lecture three years ago, Niall FitzGerald, then
chairman of Unilever*, told the story of their
Country Soups. Sales were poor and getting poorer
– and he'd been asked to authorise a significant
expenditure in order to upgrade the quality of
Country Soups' ingredients. On instinct, he asked to
see the list of ingredients as it had been 20 years
earlier, when the brand had been strong. His
instinct was right. The list of ingredients then had
been almost exactly the list of ingredients it was now
proposed, at considerable expense, to reinstate. In
between, a succession of profit-conscious brand
managers, believing the sizzle to be more important
than the steak, had slowly and furtively whittled
away at intrinsic quality, telling themselves that each
change was so negligible as to be undetectable. So it
was that a soup, calling itself Country Soup, with all
the hoped-for associations of rural, straight-from-

*See Posh Spice & Persil

130

Mother-Earth reality, had been persistently stripped of the evidence that would have given those associations legitimacy. It did not go undetected.

Don't Try to Fake Authenticity

Over-enthusiasm for sizzle marketing is more dangerous today than ever because there's a growing and clearly detectable popular thirst for what is usually summed up as authenticity. Increasingly, people like to know the provenance of what they buy. Countries of origin and regions of origin provide valued reassurance. Knowledge of a brand's history and the people behind it can contribute a great deal to belief in the brand's worth.

Artificiality is suspect; authenticity welcome: as long, of course, as the authenticity is authentic.

In many countries, this emerging search for authenticity has favoured the rise and rise of farmers' markets and farm shops. A new farm shop opened last year in the county of Wiltshire in England.

The shop was housed in a well-converted old barn.
There was a stripped wooden floor, the fruit and
vegetables were displayed in wicker baskets and
details of local produce were hand-lettered on a
blackboard. The place absolutely reeked of
authenticity.

The home-made steak & kidney pie looked
particularly appetising – so we bought one and had
it for supper that evening. The steak inside the pie
was meagrely distributed and far from tender. My
wife found two small pieces of kidney. I found
none.

To many of us English, the steak & kidney pie is the
embodiment of authentic, basic country food. No
factory, we think, and no hypermarket, could ever
replicate its rich abundance, its melting, meaty
generosity. And now here, having inflated our hopes
and expectations, was this mean-spirited apology for
a pie; this mockery of a pie; this shameless rip-off
impostor of a pie. And the fact that we'd bought it

from a converted barn with stripped wooden floors made its duplicity doubly offensive. Inauthentic authenticity both attracts and deserves more condemnation than cheerful, unapologetic artificiality. All the farm shop's energy and investment had been expended on the sizzle: that, they believed, was all the punters cared about. The steak (and in this case, of course, also the kidney) had been cynically downgraded in pursuit of an extra penny's profit.

We have not patronised that farm shop since.

Brand As Clip-Joint

Over the last few years, whole books have been written about the importance to brands of creating and maintaining Trust. The arguments hardly need reiterating. Leading people to expect authenticity and then cheating them of it is as good a way as any of demolishing trust: it's brand as clip-joint, recklessly forfeiting future custom in pursuit of a quick buck today.

But not all those who write about the value of trust make it absolutely clear what they mean by that word; and here it's helpful to return to Professor Schwartz and *The Paradox of Choice*.

In his opening chapter, he chronicles his experience at his local 'modest' supermarket. "Returning to the food shelves, I could choose from among 230 soup offerings, including 29 different chicken soups. There were 26 varieties of instant mashed potatoes, 75 different instant gravies, 120 pasta sauces." Leaving the supermarket, he steps into his local consumer electronics store and discovers 45 different car stereo systems, 42 different computers, 27 different printers, 110 different televisions and 85 different telephones, excluding cell phones.

Looked at academically, and ignoring for a moment that limitless human ability to cope when confronted with apparently unmanageable complexity, you can see why Schwartz contends that such a bewilderment of choice 'tyrannizes' us. But every day, of course, human beings do manage the unmanageable.

Consumers Out-Source, Too

No general can personally manage an army of 50,000 men. No chief executive can personally manage a company of twice that number in 100 different countries. No reader can make an informed assessment of all 10 million works of fiction in print before deciding which three to take on holiday. Yet generals and CEOs and readers somehow maintain their sanity and their ability to function – because what we all do, of course, sometimes consciously and sometimes instinctively, is delegate.

The general has no more than a dozen people reporting to him. The CEO works with a small executive committee. And readers rely on their experience of a limited number of authors, subjects, reviewers and publishers.

Call it delegation or sub-contracting or out-sourcing: the principle is the same. The management of our lives is possible only through delegation; and delegation is made possible only by the existence of trust.

So in order to make satisfactory decisions, we do not need to have first-hand knowledge of every one of Professor Schwartz's 230 soups, 120 pasta sauces or 45 car stereos. Those who believe that brands are invented by companies and imposed from above on gullible citizens wilfully ignore the obvious truth: that brands (including of course corporate brands and retail brands and media brands) provide an indispensable consumer service. They are our trusted lieutenants to whom we confidently delegate and who impose some sort of order on our otherwise chaotic shopping lists.

So, in the end, it all seems to come together. Marketing conditions change and we need to be aware of those changes. But since those conditions

136

apply to our competitors as well as ourselves, this doesn't mean to say that marketing is getting harder; simply that the prizes for getting things right are even more glittering.

As choice continues to multiply, we will continue to delegate more, to subcontract more, and we will put our trust only in trustworthy names: authentic names, of demonstrable intrinsic quality. The sizzle will still get our nostrils flaring with anticipation – but if we're ever cheated of the steak & kidney, we will be vindictive until the end of time.

Why is a Good Insight
Like a Refrigerator?

Here is an Insight: *"Product satisfaction arises less
from inherent construction and performance than
from consumers' internalised perceptions of personal
utility."*

You may have found it faintly familiar; and – when
you finally worked out what it meant – more than
faintly obvious. What you won't have found it to be
is exhilarating, inspiring, memorable, actionable,
evocative. You will not have been tempted to repeat
it to colleagues or include it in your next internal
newsletter. Certainly, it contains a truth – and an
important truth at that; but it just sits there.

Between 40 and 50 years ago, Professor Theodore
Levitt famously told his Harvard Business School

students: "People don't want quarter-inch drills. They want quarter-inch holes." It's been quoted a million times ever since and enlightened generations of marketing people. But what if Professor Levitt had chosen to say this:

"Product satisfaction arises less from inherent construction and performance than from consumers' internalised perceptions of personal utility." (Doesn't improve with repetition, does it?)

His diligent students would have noted it down; but it would never have been quoted and it would have enlightened nobody.

Whether from their research companies or their communications agencies, marketing companies today are unanimous in demanding insights. There seems to be no universal agreement on what an insight is but a reasonable definition would seem to be something like this:

"A new understanding, probably of human behaviour or attitude, as a result of which action may be taken and an enterprise more efficiently conducted."

The call for insights is natural. To return to Levitt's dictum, marketing companies don't want research; they want enlightenment. Conventional market research, professionally conducted, can paint an invaluable picture of the immediate past; but companies also need help in forging their futures. That's what lies behind the demand for insights – but not all insights are equal. They come in two very different styles and with very different values. There are low-potency insights and there are high-potency insights.

"Product satisfaction arises less from inherent construction and performance than from consumers' internalised perceptions of personal utility" is a low-

potency insight. *"People don't want quarter-inch drills. They want quarter-inch holes"* is a high-potency insight.

And the difference in value between these two has nothing to do with the intrinsic observation itself. Both assertions contain the same truth. In fact, to be really pedantic, the low-intensity version, when scrutinised carefully, actually turns out to be more accurate and more comprehensive than the Levitt version – because, of course, people don't want quarter-inch holes any more than they want quarter-inch drills. They want bookshelves or wall lamps or rabbit hutches. The low-potency version, with its reference to "consumers' internalised perceptions of personal utility" neatly covers this point: but at what cost. Literal accuracy prevails but inspiration is smothered. Where the low-potency insight utterly fails is in instant, heart-lifting revelation. It never elicits that immediate, exultant response: "Yes, of course! That's exactly how it is!"

142

Bold hypothesis

This is familiar stuff to all creative agencies. The account planner or strategist who comes up with an immaculate and scrupulously accurate relief map of the brand and its market – and absolutely nothing else – will not be greatly loved by the creative group. By definition, a good creative brief contains a bold hypothesis. To generate hypotheses you need to speculate: you need to progress from the known to the unknown. But you cannot paint the future in the colours of the past. Other people's imaginations need to be engaged, excited, signed on as accomplices. And the choice of the language you use is not arbitrary and inconsequential; for an insight to have real potency, the language in which it is couched is at least as important as the inner truth itself. For an insight to have real potency, literal accuracy is less important than its power to evoke.

A long time ago, I wrote a short piece about brands in which I said: "People build brands as birds build nests, from scraps and straws we chance upon." And I've been extremely gratified ever since to find this phrase quite widely picked up and approvingly quoted.

I've also been amazed that no one has ever challenged it; because, as I can now exclusively reveal for the first time, it's demonstrably untrue on at least two counts.

As every ornithologist knows, birds don't build their nests from scraps and straws they chance upon; they know exactly what raw materials they need and they set out deliberately to find them: mud, sheep's wool, moss, twigs – are all knowingly sought out and secured. That is how birds build nests; but is not, of course, at all how consumers build brands.

Nor do we, as consumers, chance upon most brand clues: they are laid in our path by the brand's owner – the packs, the promotions, the price, the advertising – in the cunning hope and expectation that the brand we thereby build will be the one we'll come to love and favour.

Had I been more responsible, more concerned with accuracy and truth, this is what I should have written all those years ago: *"Stakeholders form the framework of brand concepts less from holistic perceptions than from the convergence of disaggregated structural elements."*

It's no new game to mock marketing language – though too much of it still continues to invite mockery. There are times when marketing language kills thought, strangles speculation, anaesthetises the imagination. While marketing jargon remains guilty of these crimes against understanding, it deserves to be mocked. But there's an even more serious point to be made.

In business, we seem to want to follow the linguistic philosophers; to believe that the rigorous researcher or the business professional deals only in matters of fact; always defines terms; and aims for the total elimination of ambiguity. In fact, of course, if every word employed is underpinned by definition, it follows that every definition employed needs to be underpinned by definition – and so on into what is called infinite regression. In the pursuit of economy and precision, we achieve instead circumlocution, opacity and chaos.

"Stepping stones for thought"

Instead, when searching for high-potency expression of sometimes complex insights, it's a great deal more fruitful to accept the limitations of language; and to agree with Arthur Koestler when he says that "Words in themselves are never completely explicit; they are merely stepping stones for thought." (It's a wonderful sentence that; not only an important insight, but an elegant example, in itself, of the very truth it contains.)

High-potency insights, because of their immediacy
– because they evoke as well as inform – behave
like the best viral ads on the internet. They are
infectious; we only have to hear them once to
remember them, to apply them, to pass them on to
others. By contrast, the low-potency insight sits
there sullenly on its PowerPoint slide, moving
absolutely nobody to enlightenment, let alone
action.

Insights framed in high-potency terms invariably
avoid the direct and the explicit. They stay close
to the original meaning of wit: communications
of great economy achieved through the use of
unexpected associations between contrasting or
disparate words or ideas. Koestler calls it
bisociation.

Metaphors, analogies and similes invite the receivers'
participation, as in a joke; so that the point is not
rifled relentlessly home but is 'seen'. Examined

147

forensically, most high-potency insights won't even be semantically accurate. That's because they work not through description but through allusion. They should, however, convey a greater truth.

Giving high potency to an insight is an intensely creative act: it requires a massive injection of imagination. As with any other creative act, it also demands an understanding of what is already in the receiver's mind; and just as importantly, what is not already in the receiver's mind. Metaphors, similes and analogies work only when the reference points are already familiar to their audience. Levitt's audience already knew about drills and holes.

Poets, of course, do it instinctively. That's why the works of Shakespeare contain so many quotations. For a short, cheap course in evocative communication, the *Oxford Dictionary of Quotations* can be highly recommended.

The origins of an insight are usually to be found in numbers. That's how we know an insight to be more than airy whim; that's how we know it has substance; that it can be tested and replicated. But, except to the supernaturally numerate, numbers seldom sing spontaneously. For the rest of us, numbers conceal enlightenment at least as effectively as jargon. That's when we need to call on words – provocative, allegorical words – to let in fresh air; to liberate the insight and give it immediate, self-evident potency. In both research companies and creative agencies, there are people we know who can effect this alchemy. They do it every time they turn dry, mechanistic market analysis, first into creative strategy and then (occasionally) into sublime creative execution. We should use them more often, consciously and deliberately, to cast the same spell on recalcitrant data.

It's no new thought to suggest that the value of an insight, the utility of an insight, is dependent not only on the originality and accuracy of that insight but at least as much on the potency of its expression. It's exactly what Alexander Pope was getting at:

"True wit is nature to advantage dress'd,
What oft was thought but ne'er so well express'd."

It is almost certainly the case that, already paid for, there's a great Aladdin's cave of knowledge out there: but as yet unlocked by consummate expression. It's as if great quantities of rough and unappealing diamonds had already been mined – and then left to moulder in a warehouse. In the real world of diamonds, of course, that would never be allowed to happen. If diamonds are to deliver their real value, they need to be cut and polished.

We mine for insights, too. And we should be as insistent as the diamond trade that, once unearthed, they be cut and polished – and made to glitter and inspire.

So to return to the beginning:

Why is a Good Insight Like a Refrigerator?

Because the moment you look into it, a light comes on.

Acknowledgements

The low-potency versions of Levitt's drill and my bird's nest aphorisms were written by the late Stephen King. A lifelong enemy of marketing jargon, he could parody it with devastating effect and I'm extremely grateful to him. I also invited him to produce a low-potency version of anything from Shakespeare. He chose the Polonius speech from Hamlet, "Neither a borrower nor a lender be . . ." "In overseas assignments it is essential to keep an appropriate and sustainably balanced credit/debit ratio. Unsecured loans may be irrecoverable and can endanger potentially profitable relationships, while sporadic borrowing inflows can conceal the underlying reality of cash flow projections."

Many of the ideas in this essay began life in a
Keynote Address to The Market Research Society
Conference, London, March 2005. The author is
the Society's current president.

Index

153

Index

Index

Index

Index

Index

Index

Index

Index

Index

Index